The Shepherds of Tenth Avenue

poems by

Allison Thorpe

Finishing Line Press
Georgetown, Kentucky

The Shepherds of Tenth Avenue

Copyright © 2018 by Allison Thorpe
ISBN 978-1-63534-784-5 First Edition
All rights reserved under International and Pan-American Copyright Conventions.
No part of this book may be reproduced in any manner whatsoever without written
permission from the publisher, except in the case of brief quotations embodied in
critical articles and reviews.

ACKNOWLEDGMENTS

The author wishes to thank these journals in which earlier versions of the
following poems first appeared:

3 Elements Journal ~ "How Much Is That Neon Lime Green Bikini in the
Window"
Citron Review ~ "Vietnam Visits the Neighborhood"
Clapboard House ~ "Attack of the Crone Woman," "Biology"
Connecticut River Review ~ "The Undead"
Dead Flowers ~ "The Table of My History"
Dirty Chai ~ "Something Wild My Way Came"
Dying Dahlia ~ "The Last Time My Mother Baked Bread"
Freshwater ~ "Skills"
Gravel Magazine ~ "My Father's War," "Good Girls Don't Scream"
Kentucky Review ~ "What Remains" (as "Summer Storm")
Kindred Magazine ~ "The House of Growing Up"
Kudzu ~ "Dolls"
Milo Review ~ "Slap"
Misfit Magazine ~ "In the Liquor Business"
Motif Vol. 4: An Anthology of Writings about Water ~ "Inheritance"
Naugatuck River Review ~ "The Summer of Cribbage with the Gypsy
Queen"
Poetry Super Highway ~ "Photo with Church Hats"
Silver Threads, Vol. 22 ~ "Attack of the Crone Woman" Reprint
South85 Journal ~ "Summer School"
Still: The Journal ~ "How to Tell Your Mother You Don't Like Knitting"
The Voices Project ~ "Aunt Willie," "Mantra at 2 a.m."

Publisher: Leah Maines
Editor: Christen Kincaid
Cover Art: Allison Thorpe
Author Photo: Allison Thorpe
Cover Design: Leah Huete

Printed in the USA on acid-free paper.
Order online: www.finishinglinepress.com
also available on amazon.com

Author inquiries and mail orders:
Finishing Line Press
P. O. Box 1626
Georgetown, Kentucky 40324
U. S. A.

Table of Contents

For Sarah and the Friday morning writers

Mantra at 2 a.m.

It's a familiar tale my father spins of my birth
How my mother, full of me, shed her water
In the gut of night
The claw of blizzard

How my father, proud new car owner,
Lurched and wallowed that shiny Plymouth
Over desolate, ice-studded roads
Toward the distant hospital

How one final skid into a vast snowdrift
Stalled their labored journey
Cutting heat and power
Safe but stranded in that arctic anarchy

How he sheltered his overcoat around us
And dashed down the bitter streets
Howling for any compassionate soul
Awake and willing his creationed quest

How in the gust and swirling dark
Greedy with snow and waiting
My mother sang us someplace warm
She sang us someplace brave

Inheritance

Your people were water folk
Quickened risers of depths
Murky and plentiful
All sinewy arms and bulk shoulders
Boated legs for heave and balance
The drag of mended fishing nets
Weathering cold until joints
Stiffened with knots
Hands becoming clawed
Instruments attached to wrists

Time and women took generations inward
Fishermen morphing to land trawlers
Preying wood rather than water
Still the hands remained busy
But never moving far from the source

You were born among cedar and sawdust
Growing with burls and levels
Distant from water, knowing only
The race over burning grains of sand
To soothe toes in the cool wetness
Feeling somehow content in the swirling
Suck of currents and tides

Some evenings you are drawn to its lonely lure
Sharing the swell and pull of the world
The drowning stun of sunsets
You sit and stare into that blue story
Heed the faith of its whispered pulse

The Neighbor's Garden

Every spring of my childhood the garden plot waited
with new loamed challenge for my father.
Weather framed our budding lives.
Tools were honed and oiled.
The old straw hat returned to peg.
With one eye skyward and the other on the house next door,
my father hovered the windows fixed for action.

My sister and I watched amazed as he and the neighbor
broke ground, sowed and watered fragile seedlings,
dueled the purity of pea blossoms, prodded the plump
of lima beans, quarreled corn that threatened rooftops,
staked roses that sang blood all summer.

Earlier and earlier the men wakened, later and later
worked the fading day, the neighbor's voice high
and hearty at each grand bloom or fruitful branch,
my father's bass-edged preen crooning color and quantity.

Lettuce, tomatoes, lilacs, currants, the men gifted
those shaded streets with their colorful harvestings.
"Extras" dominated dinner tables. Women baked
squash pies, stewed up apples and pears, stuffed and
preserved those drowsy nutmeg and cinnamon days,
lingered the scent of dill long into the night.

My father didn't garden the year the neighbor died,
the black crumbly miracles left to dust and bramble.
He said he wanted it that way, liked the idea
of earth lingering, savored watching the sky instead
for the quickened bloom of birds.

The Undead

I grew up among the undead
those sepia strangers
blank faced gypsies
who framed walls and cluttered shelves

we dusted them weekly like religion
shined the immaculate visions
of our past bestowing them
the life we didn't tithe ourselves

ladies in high-necked gowns
lace and ribbons jewels
sober men in worn suits
and well parted hair
working women glued to their aprons

rooting us by genes
with names like
Elnora
August
Wilhemena
Gerhard

their dark eyes keening
strangled journeys
wide waters
promise-laden lands

their frozen stories following us
through parties and dinners
watching our sleep with envy
their secrets kindling
the muted air around us

The Last Time My Mother Baked Bread

I had a child's impatience
for the sweet rising—
crayons, dolls, tinker toys
only ticked the minutes—
then the baking's
agonizing dawdle.
She read me through
an eternity of cooling
with the promised
crusty first slice
when we heard the slur
and stumble on the stairs,
sensed the sour change
before he appeared,
the room suddenly
thick in his boozy musk,
the fragrant loaf
small in his roughened hands,
fingers slowly
mashing the bread
and throwing the pieces
at my mother.
In that stilled silence,
we heard his car
screech down the road.

For weeks after
she cleaned the room,
random crumbs
would stab my bare feet,
hard and sharp
reminders
of love.

Photo with Church Hats

My mother insisted on the outing
Roused us like roosters
Slathering us in Sunday finery
(We were not church people)

Plopped the wide flat saucers
On our startled heads—
Surely the early pattern for Frisbees
Those hats could scare any doorway

Stiff scratchy ribbon hard tied
To keep our whiny chins in line
Lace flowed like holy water
And plastic petals faked a life

Below that blessed gauding
My sister and I wriggled
Agonized faces like sour
Pumpkins missing teeth

Maybe Mother craved miracles—
The hallowing hymnals or strict pews
Some stained glass Jesus
To stray my father from his habits

Photo blurred in haste or hate
My mother's face so hopeful
It took me years to realize
The picture was not about our hats

Attack of the Crone Woman

A pocket full of names we had for her—
hag, witch, scarecrow, she-devil, old bat—
but crone ruled, rolled the mouth joyously.
She was someone's grandmother
or just a woman renting an upstairs flat.
No one cared.

She threw wooden clothespins
from her second story window
if our street play got too loud,
was lethal with her cane
if we rode our bicycles too close.

She wore a bright plastic flower
above her right ear, grey hair marshaled
into a strict bun, and faded
black dresses with lace collars
circling a withered chicken neck.
We told her off from behind the garage,
imitated her bent back and rigid shuffle,
tamed her ugly ways in our dreams.

One morning when we haunted curbs
sharply arguing whose turn it was at go-kart,
we saw her come out on her upstairs porch,
her hair wet and knee-length loose.
Gently she combed the sun into those locks,
drying a silver waterfall shimmering
with glittered light, strands binding
us to her alluring web,
our mouths silenced by the silk
of so much beauty.

Skills

wood ripened
in his hands:
table
bird house
doll crib
I brought him lemonade
and danced in his smile

but time tempered
that light
for reasons
too complex
for children
his silence
grew edges
and lemons
crafted into
harder blends

in his workroom
garden
garage
he steadily retreated
from us
until what was left
of self
sank and settled
like a ship
to the bottom
of a bottle

The Table of My History

It belonged to Grandma Phyllis
Or maybe Great Aunt Gertrude
Anyway it had lived in the family dining room
For as long as I can remember
Well polished in myth—
It crossed the prairie in covered wagon
Came from Texas on the back of a mule
Sailed the Mayflower
Or maybe it survived dust storms
Wild animal attacks
Outlived famine and plague—
The Paul Bunyan of tables
Thick round mahogany top
Sturdy pillared base
Bulky struts with outturned ends
Leaves enough to extend the surface
For any birthday or reunion

My father hated it
Tried to stain it with coffee mugs
And cigarettes too long in the ash
The solid pedestal thumped his knees
Curved braces barked his shins
Upturned feet nipping his ankles
Left little room to tuck his long legs

After work and too many beers
Or maybe shots
Or laughs with familiar strangers
He would bring that fun home
Hurl it through the doorway
Stinking and swaying his merriment
Bounce if off the hall pictures
And around the living room walls
Then slam his fists into the table
We all hid behind closed doors
Terrified of too much joy

Mother would usually sneak out
To window shop, possibly seeing
A happy woman in the reflection
We left by the back door
To blast music on stoops
Or maybe play kick the can
In the twilight of forgetting

One Saturday he over-spiced his coffee
And took a saw to the table
Carried the top down to his basement workshop
Or maybe he rolled it down the stairs
Covered it with tools
And clamped a vise to the edge
We never found the bottom
When we came home
A folding card table stood in its place
Mother sitting stunned
She slowly walked into the guest bedroom
And closed the door
We didn't see her for years
Clothes were cleaned and piled on our beds
School lunches, dinners appeared
As if some magical genie had landed

Sometimes we would creep down the silence
And find father in his workshop
Staring at the table top
As if unsure how it had gotten there
Or maybe as if it held the heart of the world

Aunt Willie

Unrepentant source of eyebrow-raising sin as I grew up,
Aunt Willie was alien to my mother and the other sisters,
1950s housewives who never wavered from family dinners,
scrubbed floors on their knees, whitened and brightened
and sacrificed their days for others.

We overheard the conversations, tantalizing words—
lover, affair, abortion—before we knew their power,
never quite sure if the women were jealous or betrayed
by her absence, her early Midwest departure
to the warmer embrace of oceans and elegance.

We saw pictures: the red plump of mouth, dark spark
of eye, long tan legs on display, proudly showing off
curves our mothers hid under aprons or high-necked ruffles,
the appeal our fathers lusted but never mentioned,
swapping Willie for Wilhelmina in her B movie credits.

Maybe they resented her strength and independence,
her attention to self long before liberation came
to kitchens or bedrooms, or wondered how a family
so solemn could spawn such an exotic mutation, one
we were taught not to be like but never understood why.

So while we grew to be the good girls, there was that
gene that made us doubt, made us roll our skirt bands up
to flash more skin, kept our hands raised long after
teachers called on all the boys, caused us to wonder
how we would look in army tanks or space ships,
to imagine a woman reaching against black sheep math,
a woman reaching toward uncommon castles,
        a woman reaching.

What Remains

The storm rose early
with crow black alarm,
snatching leaves and limbs,
swirling and yanking and whipping—
a mad scientist in the yard,
a tantrumed child tossing
curbside garbage cans,
a lion roaring and snarling
bloodied meat.

Fearful and excited we watched
the spectacle from an upstairs window.
A sudden shudder killed the electricity,
mother rushing us to the basement,
lighting a thousand candles along the way,
prayers fierce under her breath.

Father came home early,
the town in hiding.
He swung his lantern,
shadows highlighting a hand
roughened with roof work
and shadowed tobacco yellow.

When my sister started crying,
he sang *What a Friend We Have in Jesus;*
when she stopped sobbing,
he sang *Purple People Eater* and *Peggy Sue.*

We didn't often see him like this:
unmarred by drink and hate.
Deep in our stomachs it startled us
almost as much as the storm.

Mother gingerly opened the big freezer,
eyebrows a knitted question,
and brought out ice cream sandwiches.
We laughed as I stammered a ghost story
overheard at Corrine's slumber party.

Despite the rage and wrath of the day,
the destruction sent down to our world
by some furious sky warlord,
I filed those hours away
in my thin family album
of treasured memories.

Years later, recalling that day
was like unearthing gold
in the mashed potatoes,
a clean joke stashed in dirty
laundry, rainbows fanning
the shuttered dark.

Dolls

One summer morning at Sandra's
we became Basement Barbies.
We bleached our hair,
brushed it into ponytails,
used a whole box of Kleenex to convince our bras,
and shuddered about in her mother's high heels.
Her little brother refused to play Ken,
disappearing into his room and locking the door.

After a week of blistered feet,
singed raw scalps,
and pissed off mothers,
we rethought our decision.

When school started in fall,
and Sandra's hair took a greenish turn,
the kids called us Alien Barbies;
while reading Shakespeare in English class,
they yelled Weird Sister Barbies;
as our hair began to grow out,
Two tone Barbies;
and when I accidentally caught a candy cane in my hair,
Peppermint Barbies.

The next summer we invested
in bikinis and boys,
trying to grow back into the girls
our mothers meant us to be.

In the Liquor Business

My father worked hard
at running up a bar tab.
Always on the job.

See his corner bar stool,
the one without a window
or sun-starved ivy.

He skipped lunch,
put in the long hours,
worked overtime.
Fierce at taking inventory—
beer, scotch, bourbon—
he stored the liquid assets
faithfully in his liver.

It was not an occupation
my mother would have chosen.
She worked two jobs to cover
the bills and his corporate
raids on her purse.

My father resented
the limited partnership,
the family who took no joy
in his staggering success.

How Much Is That Neon Lime Green Bikini in the Window?

I never wanted anything more.
It sang to me like a thousand sirens.
For the moment it belonged to a curvy blonde
pony-tailed mannequin holding a beach ball.
Two hunk plastic males leaned on a blanket
staring up at her in open admiration.
Someone had scattered sand
on the showroom floor for reality.

I babysat all June and July,
carted home groceries for Mrs. Wilson,
cut grass and washed windows
until I had that bikini in my hands.
I couldn't wait to wear it,
dazzling all at the shore.

That grand day of unveiling
I walked the beach, my short brown hair
in a somewhat ponytail,
no curves—I was flat as a Kansas prairie—
but I carried a beach ball and a flirty smile.
All afternoon I strolled the sands,
dipped my toes alluringly in the gentle waves,
flaunted that neon limeness,
ignored all the looks in my direction,
fended off two annoying kids
who tried to grab my ball
until a woman pointed at me and said,
Maybe you should put on a shirt.
You're getting awfully red.
But I was having the day of my life,
the day I had fantasized for months.

Reality introduced me to agony,
unwelcome fans now stalking my every move.
My clothes scraped a sandpaper nightmare on skin.
Even my hair betrayed me, slashing
my neck like some horror movie villain.
Finally at home, I screamed
as each shower droplet battered
any last vestige of teenage dignity.
I looked with loathing
at the soggy neon limpness
huddled on the bathroom floor.
Pride and the sun had branded
its image onto my sorrowed skin.

For weeks the image of that suit
possessed my scorched body,
throbbed the sleepless nights.
I wore a thin baggy dress
and stayed in my room.
My eyes consumed every tear.
I became friends with the moon,
inhaling that kind silver coolness
and wanting nothing.

My Father's War

Life began with Pearl Harbor, he always said,
tossing away his youth like hole shabby socks,
while he stuffed our childhood with D-Day,
Normandy, Omaha Beach, Saint Lo,
names like a reunion of familiar
relatives we had never met.

Midway, beachhead, kamikaze,
woven into our hours: a rug
that covered us at night, dreaming
not of sugar plums, but battalions and bazookas.
Guadalcanal, Gestapo, Iwo Jima
joining the family at dinner, crowding
the small table, demanding more potatoes,
devouring all the corn and meatloaf.

Military conventions each summer posed
as vacations where we swam and played
with other children while Dunkirk and Vichy
shrieked loudly in the background,
where the wives window shopped
Luftwaffe and victory gardens,
and the men bought blitzkriegs
and panzers at the bar,
none of us noticing father's
own slow slide into the bottle.

Was it during the story of Wake Island?
The Third Reich? Battle of the Bulge?
Was it the sameness, the tameness
of life after war, house with mortgage?
Maybe the payments on the old Plymouth?
The weekly check never quite stretching?
Wife and daughters never quite measuring up
to that brotherhood born of men?

Summer School

It was a job I didn't want
But one my mother scolded
I was lucky to get
    Lucky to be hired this summer
    Lucky to be making money at your age
    Lucky to be spending time together
    Lucky lucky lucky

I did odd jobs at the printing plant
Where she slaved away her days
Watching the colorful inked pages
Fill up my summer dance card
    Calendars
    Wedding announcements
    Church bulletins
    Store coupons
They flew around the plant
Like frantic gaudy bats

Around me women of my mother's age
Sleeveless shirts and flappy arms
Huffed and shrieked their secrets
    Open the windows it's too hot
    Close the door I'm freezing
    Get me an ice cold soda
    Fetch my sweater, Dear

The women fluctuated the hours
Between the machines' buzz and hum
Their *open/close* its own constant droning
A time of clasped cardigans
And hurricane force fans
They smelled of ink and cigarettes
And poked at my shyness
Hinting the trek through womanhood
Yet to be realized

When the windows were open
I would gaze out
At the A & W Root Beer stand
Across the busy road
Like some distant wishing star
Carloads of teenagers spewing fun
Around the picnic tables outside

When the windows were closed
I reflected on the machine song
The tango of paper and wisdom
Among the women
The colorful dust of luck settled

Slap

Johnny Bishop asked me to the movies.
He had Elvis hair, so I went.
After popcorn and candy
and his arm along the back of my chair,
he walked me slowly home.
Under the muted porch light,
he leaned over to kiss me like he was
Moondoggie and I was Gidget
before saying he would call me again
and wandering off into the night.
It was as dreamy as any romantic movie,
so I forgot about survival.

In real life,
one quickly learns to read the signs:
a sudden rattle of the doorknob,
the way his foot thudded on the stairs,
the slur of the word.
I had 30 wonderful inattentive seconds
thinking about Johnny Bishop's kiss
before the side of my face exploded.

I had heard that sound once from a rifle
when men had come to scare
hordes of blackbirds from the trees.
It held a crack, a stillness, an echo.

The world went dumb for long seconds
until breath came gushing back
through thick air and stunned amazement,
then I ran for my bedroom.
There was no talking to my father
in those moments,
no asking *What did I do wrong?*
Why did you hit me?
There was just a door and a lock.

Mother came later with ice
to deaden the sting,
the angry redness.
She soothed my hair
and sang me down to a troubled sleep,
but neither cold nor lullaby
could ease that brand of pain.
In my world of long ago and yesterday,
before disorders were dissected and treated,
away from any close family
and ashamed to go to friends,
wariness and concealment were our saviors.
The minister came to the house a time or two,
but father never let him in.

I know Johnny Bishop didn't understand
when I said no the next time
he called to ask me out,
my blushing cheek
still raw and unforgiven.

Vietnam Visits the Neighborhood

The sky purpled on the day he died
and the sun went orange to bed.
I remember my mother had made
pork chops and sauerkraut,
their twang shaping the mood
when I opened the kitchen door.

She rose from the table, wiping the tears—
my father always made her cry—
but she held a darker sadness this time.
Vonnie Thompson she said.
No one was happy when his number came up.
His girlfriend begged him to go to Canada.

I remembered him tying my shoes
on the way to grade school,
his thin fingers flying over
the tight double knots,
the way he caressed a basketball
before sending it home to hoop,
who saved me a dance at prom,
his hand firm on the small of my back.

But everyone had their own story:
He had such a great smile
What a kind heart
The longest legs you've ever seen
Good head on his shoulders
Those feet could soar on the court
until I began to wonder
if we saw people in body parts

Over the years his face
has blurred to shadows,
voice a lost music,
walk fading to horizon,
hands now dry and silent,
but in my mind busy, busy.

Good Girls Don't Scream

I wanted to be like Janis
Or Grace on a good day
Toss my hair around
Wear thin rainbow tops
With no bra
Not because I didn't need one
But because I was cool
Wanted to have some
Brown-eyed guitar player
Lust my sway and step
Dance with the beat
Of a bare-chested drummer
Wanted to stomp a stage
And wail a note well into tomorrow

But there was enough
Drama at home
So I was just a girl
Who stayed in on weekends
Who did all her homework
Who wrote in a diary
And dreamed about Fabian

The Summer of Cribbage with the Gypsy Queen

We were introduced at a party.
She was looking for a pigeon
and I cooed.

She met me in the park every week
to beat me at cribbage, my losses
supporting her rum habit.

Her aura held such an exotic wilderness,
my concentration sat on a back burner
slowly roasting wrinkles from my brain.

She was a tank of tropical fish,
a Mediterranean sunset,
a box of crayons on Christmas morning.

Silver bangles played her arm like a symphony
each time she stroked a card or moved a peg.
Her ears sprouted peacock feathers

that paraded her stark blonde hair,
stoking the flash of wide dark eyes.
A low cut white blouse kept no one wondering.

Her ankle flowing skirts made even
the dingy park benches shine like fine art.
I was the blue jean and t-shirt kind of girl.

After the games, for $1 extra
she colored my palm
with the most marvelous lies,

her smooth red fingernail
tracking heart and fate,
curve and cross.

She smelled lightly of oranges and musk.
I smelled like yeast and bread dough
from the bakery where I worked.

She lived with an older man
in a renovated warehouse by the bridge.
I lived with my parents.

Her mystical flounce and dare
fluttered around us and landed on me
like butterflies or volcanic ash.

I thought about streaking my hair,
donning some peony bright dress,
high sleek boots and granny glasses.

One Saturday in a small boutique
I tried on that possible me.
Nearby, a boy prodded his sister and laughed.

Like a waking coma patient or drowning goat,
I surfaced the clear air and stopped meeting her,
avoided the park altogether.

Instead, I bought a toe ring
and traced my own lifelines,
accepting the wilderness of my ordinary.

Biology

Slick warren of rock
Water with no conclusion

The old town quarry
Lurks your chary passage

Family leisure by day
Teenage taunt at night

The knowing boys
Bring their blankets

And urge your hesitancy
Into the moony depths

You leave your worries
Tucked with your underwear

Glide skin on downy skin
Loose the unexpected shudder

Your voice: one fluid echo
Such an organic drowning

Something Wild My Way Came

He scattered his revolution
Like bird seed
And I, a lonely wren,
Pecked and pecked

I jumped to his waiting hand
As we marched the cause
Braved police batons
And flew from tear gas

I ruffled with his protest
Stop the war
Save the whales
Ban the bomb

His frantic energy swallowed
Eased my smaller battles at home
Even in sleep
He had no quiet moments

I sang his troubled brow
Nuzzled the butter hair
Kissed the shrugging shoulder
Of that restless force

Before I met him
I was a flat tire
An empty cereal bowl
A forgotten birthday cake

Wrapped in his arms
Amid the rant and swirl
I felt like feather, like bone,
In the crave of the storm

How To Tell Your Mother You Don't Like Knitting

It teaches wonderful skills for a girl:
focus, determination, patience.

She punctuates the air with one needle,
a green metallic exclamation point,

a shiny lightning rod offering
a straight path to heaven.

She shows you again and again
the simple intricacies of knit and purl,

of cast on and loop over loop,
clicking her joy like a demented robot.

Garter stitch coils like a snake
ready to sting your startled fingers.

Seed stitch surely sprouting
some garden from hell.

Tell her that your primary focus
is on Billy Johnson's ripe lips,

that your determination
is to get out of this laid-up town,

that you are 16 and hold no room
for that kind of patience in your life.

Decades later, you are back
opening the trunk she left you.

The green marbling of the scarf
gives color to your black dress.

You wrap the afghan around
your shoulders to calm the chill,

the shaking that will not stop.

The House of Growing Up

lies on some distant corner of my mind.
An invisible hand has brightened the gray
edged window trim, a strange man
mows the yard, and a giggled blonde child
plays on the swing set I always hungered.

I watch from a car across the street
and a lifetime of histories.
A part of me begs to see my old room.
Are the 45s still spread over the desk?
Does the blue prom dress hang in the closet?
Is there a diary hidden among the socks?

A treasured sea shell topped my dresser,
an early morning vacation find, carried
from its sunny sandy leisure to this chilly
house, this Midwestern stillness.
On sad nights, those rage-swirled
moments of fist and fury
heard through papery walls,
I held that thin skeleton to my ear,
distracted by the faint whoosh, the primal
language of shipwrecks and tidal waves,
that lure of mermaids and motion.

My fingers would marvel the spine-laced
intricacies and smooth inner elegance,
imagining the warm churning forces
that had carved its fragile legend.

Grains of that longing girl rest now
in the journeyed woman who lingers,
who silently traces her icy past
on the fog-fevered car window,
a woman who eventually drives off
to warmer receptions, the whoosh
of leaving still deep in her ears.

Allison Thorpe is the author of *Thoughts While Swinging a Wild Child in a Green Mesh Hammock* (Janze Publications), *Swooning and Other Fun Art Forms* (NFSPS Chapbook Winner), *What She Sees* (White Knuckle Press), and *Dorothy's Glasses* (Finishing Line Press). Recent poetry appears in *Still: The Journal, Stonecoast Review, Solidago, Appalachian Heritage, Pine Mountain Sand & Gravel, Pleiades, Tipton Poetry Journal, Roanoke Review,* and anthologies *Forgotten Women* (Grayson Books) and *Nasty Women Poets* (Lost Horse Press). She works as a writing mentor at Carnegie Center for Literacy and Learning and serves on the board of the Kentucky Women Writers Conference. Memberships include Kentucky State Poetry Society, LPS, Poezia, Ellie's Writers, and Buddha Girls. She lives in Lexington, KY.

www.ingramcontent.com/pod-product-compliance
Lightning Source LLC
LaVergne TN
LVHW051611080426
835510LV00020B/3239